Top 10 best Bedtime Stories for Children: A Collection of Night Time Tales with Great Morals to Help Children and Toddlers

Go to Sleep Feeling relax, and Have a Good Relaxing Night's Sleep with Beautiful Dreams.

The Apostle Paul

Before his change to the confidence of Christ, Paul was called Saul, and he abused the Christians, accepting that they were doing insidiously and that he should rebuff them for it.

The transformation of Saul

The abuse of Paul

In any case, while he was amidst these abuses, and as he was traveling toward Damascus one day, he saw abruptly at early afternoon, a light sparkling in the sky which was more noteworthy than the light of the sun, and he and all that were with him tumbled to the earth in awe and wonder. Then, at that point, Saul heard a voice addressing him and saying, "Saul, Saul, for what reason do you mistreat Me?" And Saul said, "Who workmanship Thou, Lord?" And the voice replied, "I'm Jesus, whom you abuse."
Then, Saul heard a voice tending to him and saying, "Saul, Saul, why do you abuse Me?" And Saul said, "Who workmanship Thou, Lord?" And the voice answered, "I'm Jesus, whom you misuse."
Be that as it may, he was oppressed in his new work as he had mistreated others, being at last taken prisoner and undermined with scourging; he announced himself a Roman resident, in any case, and hence protected from such treatment, and continued

transparently admitting his confidence and recounting his transformation, and he pursued for assurance to the Roman
sovereign.

He was then placed on board a boat as a detainee to be taken to Rome.
 While they were adrift a savage tempest came up, and Paul cautioned the mariners that they were in extraordinary peril; yet they would not pay attention to him.

 Finally, the boat was destroyed, already being provided reason to feel ambiguous about shoreward an island, whither they had been conveyed, sticking to sheets and broken bits of the boat.

The primitive individuals of the island treated them compassionate, building a fire that they may dry their dress and get warm; for it was cold and they were, obviously, soaked.

The men were extremely happy to be protected again; yet something bizarre occurred after a bit: Paul got together an armful of sticks to put upon the fire, and as he put them upon the blazes, a snake, which is a sort of toxic snake, emerged from the pack and clung to his hand; he shook it off into the fire, nonetheless, with practically no indication of dread.

The wreck of Paul

The people who were about him felt that the hand would enlarge and that Paul would pass on from the impacts of the nibble, and they watched him intently, accepting that this inconvenience was shipped off him as a discipline for his wrongdoings. However, no underhanded outcomes came from the injury, and afterward the savages thought he was a divine being and viewed him with extraordinary regard.
Paul and the ones who were with him stayed upon the island for a very long time. Toward the finish of that time, they disappeared in a boat, at last arriving at Rome, where the detainees were surrendered to the specialists; yet Paul was permitted to reside without help from anyone else, with just a trooper to monitor him, and sooner or later he called the central men of the Jews together and explained to them why he was there and lectured them the Word of God. His proclaiming was gotten by some with confidence; however, others didn't accept.

The Story of Stephen, the First Martyr

In the New Testament, in the book of Acts, you will figure out how the individuals from the congregation in Jerusalem gave their cash unreservedly to help poor people. This free giving prompted inconvenience, as the congregation became so quick; for a portion of the widows who were poor were cruised by, and their companions submitted questions to the missionaries. The twelve missionaries assembled the entire church, and said:

"It isn't well that we should divert beside lecturing and encouraging the expression of God to find a seat at tables and give out cash. Yet, brethren, browse among yourselves seven great men; men who have the Spirit of God and are savvy, and we will give this work to them; with the goal that we can invest our energy in petition and in lecturing the gospel."

This arrangement was satisfying to all the congregation and they picked seven men to assume responsibility for the gifts of individuals, and to see that they were shipped off the people who were out of luck. The main man picked was Stephen, a man loaded with confidence and of the Spirit of God; and with him were Philip and five other great men. These seven men they brought before the witnesses; and the messengers laid their hands on their heads, separating them for their work of really focusing on poor people.
Yet, Stephen did more than to take care of the poor ones. He started to lecture the good news of Christ, and to lecture with so much power as caused each one who heard him to feel reality. Stephen saw before some other man in the congregation saw, that the good news of Christ was not for Jews just, but rather was for all men; that everything men may be saved if they could have confidence in Jesus; and this extraordinary truth Stephen started to lecture with all his power. Such lecturing as this, that men who were not Jews may be saved by having faith in Christ, drove a significant number of the Jews exceptionally mad. They called every one individual who were not Jews "Gentiles," and they viewed them with disdain and contempt; yet they couldn't answer the words that Stephen expressed. They animated up individuals and the rulers, and set them against Stephen, and finally, they held onto Stephen, and brought him before the extraordinary committee of the rulers. They shared with the rulers:
"This man is continuously talking insidious words against the Temple and illegal of Moses. We have heard him say that Jesus of Nazareth will obliterate this spot, and will change the laws that Moses provided for us!"

This was part of the way obvious and incompletely bogus; yet no falsehood is just about as unsafe as that which has a little truth with it. Then, at that point, the consecrated minister shared with Stephen:

The martyrdom of Stephen

"Are these things so?" Furthermore, as Stephen rose up to answer the consecrated cleric, generally fixed their eyes upon him; and they saw that his face was sparkling, like it was the substance of a holy messenger. Then, at that point, Stephen started to discuss the extraordinary things that God had accomplished for his kin Israel before; how he had called Abraham, their dad, to go forward into another land; how he had given them incredible men, as Joseph, and Moses, and the prophets. He showed them how the Israelites had not been dedicated to God, who had given them such brilliant favors. Then, at that point, Stephen said: "You are a group with hard hearts and solid necks, who won't submit to the expressions of God and his Spirit. As your dads did, so you do, likewise. Your dads killed the prophets whom God shipped off them; and you have killed Jesus, the Righteous One!"

As they heard these things, they ended up being so irate against Stephen, that they ground on him with their teeth, similar to wild monsters. Be that as it may, Stephen, brimming with the Holy Spirit, gazed upward toward paradise with his sparkling face; and he saw the brilliance of God, and Jesus remaining on God's right hand, and he said: "I see a downpour began, and the Son of man remaining on the right hand of God!"
In any case, they shouted out with irate voices, surged upon him, and hauled him out of the committee room, and outside the mass of the city. Also, there they tossed stones upon him to kill him, while Stephen was stooping down among the falling stones, and imploring:
"Ruler Jesus, accept my soul! Ruler, lay not this wrongdoing toward them!"
Furthermore, when he had said this, he nodded off in death, the first to be killed for the good news of Christ.

The Story of the Empty Tomb

After Jesus was taken before the esteemed minister where he was criticized and individuals spat upon him, he was taken before the Roman Governor, Pontius Pilate, who managed over Judea. He heard their grievances, yet didn't track down any reason for killing him. However, finally he respected their requests, despite the fact that he pronounced Jesus was honest of all off-base.

Jesus was beaten

Thus Pontius Pilate, the Roman lead representative, provided order that Jesus should bite the dust by the cross. The Roman fighters then, at that point, took Jesus and beat him most savagely; and afterward drove him out of the city to the spot of death. This was a spot called "Golgotha" in the Jewish language, "Calvary" in that of the Romans; the two words signifying "The Skull Place."

Jesus with the cross

With the officers, left the city an incredible horde of individuals; some of them foes of Jesus, happy to see him endure; others of them companions of Jesus, and the ones who had helped him, presently sobbing as they saw him, all covered with his blood and going out to pass on. However, Jesus went to them and said:

Jesus crucified

"Girls of Jerusalem, don't sob for me, however sob for yourselves and for your kids. For the days are coming when they will count those blissful who have no little ones to be killed; when they will wish that the mountain may fall on them, and the slopes may cover them, and conceal them from their adversaries!"
They had attempted to make Jesus bear his own cross, yet before long observed that he was excessively frail from his sufferings, and couldn't convey it.
They seized on an approaching out man of the country into the city, a man named Simon, and they made him convey the cross to its place at Calvary.

It was the custom among the Jews to provide for men going to bite the dust by the cross some medication to stifle their sentiments, with the goal that they would not endure so significantly. They offered this to Jesus, yet when he had tasted it and observed what it was, he would not take it. He realized that he would kick the bucket, however he wished to have his psyche clear, and to get how was treated information exchanged, despite the fact that his sufferings may be more noteworthy.

At the spot Calvary, they laid the cross down, extended Jesus upon it, and drove nails through his hands and feet to secure him to the cross; and afterward they stood it upstanding with Jesus upon it. While the troopers were accomplishing this loathsome work, Jesus appealed to God for them to God, saying: "Father, pardon them; for they know not what they are doing."

The fighters likewise took the garments that Jesus had worn, providing for everyone an article of clothing. However, when they came to his underwear, they observed that it was woven and had no creases; so, they said, "Let us not tear it, yet cast parcels for it, to see who will have it." So, at the foot of the cross the officers tossed parts for the article of clothing of Christ.

Two men who had been burglars and had been condemned to kick the bucket by the cross, were driven out to bite the dust simultaneously with Jesus. One was put on a cross at his right side, and the other at his left; and to cause Jesus to show up as the most horrendously terrible, his cross remained in the center. Over the head of Jesus on his cross, they submitted, by Pilate's structure, a sign, on which was composed:

"This is Jesus of Nazareth, The King of the Jews."

This was written in three dialects; in Hebrew, which was the language of the Jews; in Latin, the language of the Romans, and in Greek. A large number individuals read this composition; however, the main ministers were not satisfied with it. They encouraged Pilate to have it transformed from "The King of the Jews" to "He said, I am King of the Jews." But Pilate would not transform it. He said:

"What I have composed, I have composed."

What's more individuals who passed by out and about, as they took a gander at Jesus on the cross, taunted at him. Some shouted to him:

"You that would obliterate the Temple and construct it in three days, save yourself. On the off chance that you are the Son of God, descend from the cross!"

What's more the ministers and recorders said:

"He saved others; however, he can't save himself. Descend from the cross, and we will trust in you!"

Also, one of the looters, who was on his own cross next to that of Jesus, participated in the cry, and said: "Assuming you are simply the Christ, save and save us!"

Today you will be with me in paradise

Be that as it may, the other looter told him: "Have you no feeling of dread toward God, to talk subsequently, while you are experiencing a similar destiny with this man? What's more we have the right to kick the bucket, however this man misunderstands sat idle." Then, at that point, this man shared with Jesus: "Ruler, recollect me when you come into your realm!"

Also, Jesus responded to him, as they were both holding tight their crosses: "To-day you will be with me in paradise. 'Before the cross of Jesus his mom was standing, loaded up with distress for her child, and next to her was one of his devotees, John, the follower whom he cherished best.

Different ladies other than his mom were there-his mom's sister, Mary the spouse of Cleophas, and a lady named Mary Magdalene, out of whom a year prior to Jesus had sent a shrewd soul. Jesus wished to give his mom, since he was leaving her, into the consideration of John, and he shared with her, as he looked from her to John: "Lady, see your child."

And afterward to John he said: "Child, see your mom."

What's more on that day John took the mother of Jesus home to his own home, and really focused on her as his own mom.

At about early afternoon, an unexpected dimness came over the land, and went on for three hours. In the early evening, when Jesus had been on the cross six hours of horrendous torment, he shouted out resoundingly words which implied:

After this he talked once more, saying, "I thirst!"

Furthermore, somebody dunked a wipe in a cup of vinegar, put it upon a reed, and provided him with a beverage of it. Then, at that point, Jesus expressed his final words upon the cross:

"It is done! Father, into thy hands I give my soul!"

And afterward Jesus kicked the bucket. Also at that point, the cloak in the Temple between the Holy Place and the Holy of Holies was destroyed by concealed hands from the top to the base. Also, when the Roman official, who had charge of the fighters around the cross, saw what had occurred, and how Jesus passed on, he said: "Clearly this was an exemplary man; he was the Son of God."

After Jesus was dead, one of the fighters, to be certain that he was done living, ran his lance into the side of his dead body; and out of the injury came pouring both water and blood.

Indeed, even among the leaders of the Jews a couple were companions of Jesus, however they didn't try to follow Jesus transparently. One of these was Nicodemus, the ruler who came to see Jesus around evening time. One more was a rich man who came from the town of Arimathea, and was named Joseph. Joseph of Arimathea went intensely in to Pilate, and requested that the body from Jesus may be given to him. Pilate pondered that he had kicked the bucket unexpectedly early, for frequently men lived on the cross a few days. In any case, when he observed that Jesus was truly dead, he gave his body to Joseph.

Then, at that point, Joseph and his companions brought down the assortment of Jesus from the cross, and enclosed it by fine material. Furthermore, Nicodemus brought a few valuable flavors, myrrh and aloes, which they wrapped up with the body. Then, at that point, they put the body in Joseph's own new burial chamber, which was a cavern uncovered from underneath the stone, in a nursery close to the spot of the cross. What's more before the launch of the cavern they moved an incredible stone.

Furthermore Mary Magdalene, and the other Mary, and a few different ladies, saw the burial chamber, and watched while they laid the assemblage of Jesus in it. On the following morning, a portion of the leaders of the Jews came to Pilate, and said:

The internment of Jesus
"Sir, we recall that that man Jesus of Nazareth, who tricked individuals, said while he was at this point alive, 'Following three days I will rise once more.'

The holy messenger at the burial place

Provide orders that the burial chamber will be watched and ensured for three days, or, in all likelihood his pupils might take his body, and afterward say, 'He is become alive once again'; and in this way even after his passing he might cause more damage than he did while he was alive."
Pilate shared with them:

The climb

"Set a watch, and make it as certain as possible."
Then, at that point, they put a seal upon the stone, so nobody may break it; and they set a watch of troopers at the entryway.
Also in the burial place, the assortment of Jesus lay from the evening of Friday, the day when he passed on the cross, to the beginning of Sunday, the primary day of the week, when he emerged from the dead and seemed unto his devotees.

Be that as it may, the most splendid day in all the world was this Sunday morning. For on that day the stone was rolled away from the burial chamber and Jesus approached from the dead to cheer his devotees. This he had let them know he would do. On this Sunday morning, Mary Magdalene and another Mary, called Salome, came to the burial place, observed the stone moved away and a holy messenger remaining by the open burial place. He let them know that Jesus was not there, but rather had risen.
A while later Jesus was with his supporters for forty days, after which he was taken up into paradise.

The Story of the Betrayal

At the foot of the Mount of Olives, close to the way past that certain point toward Bethany, there was a plantation of olive trees, called "The Garden of Gethsemane." " "Gethsemane" signifies "oil press." Jesus frequently went to this spot with his supporters, in view of its calm shade. At this nursery, he halted, and outside he left eight of his followers, telling them, "Stay here while I head inside and ask."

Jesus in the garden

The flesh is weak

He took with him the three anointed ones, Peter, James, and John, and went inside the plantation. Jesus realized that soon Judas would be there with a band of men to hold onto him; that in a couple of hours he would be beaten, and stripped, and drove out to pass on. The prospect of what he was to endure happened upon him and filled his spirit with misery. He shared with Peter, James, and John:
"My spirit is loaded up with distress, a distress that nearly kills me. Remain here and watch while I am asking."
He went somewhat further among the trees, flung himself downward on the ground, and shouted out:
"O my father, assuming it be conceivable, let this cup die from me; in any case, not as I will, but rather as thou will!"

So sincere was his inclination thus incredible his experiencing that there emerged upon his face extraordinary drops of sweat like blood, falling upon the ground. Subsequent to appealing to God for a period, he ascended from the earth and went to his three educates, and thought that they are largely snoozing. He awaked them, and shared with Peter: "What, could you not watch with me 60 minutes? Watch and ask that you may not go into allurement. The soul for sure is willing, yet the tissue is feeble."

He left them, went a second time into the forest, fell all over, and supplicated once more, saying:

"O my father, in the event that this cup can't die, and I should drink it, then, at that point, thy will be finished."

He came back again to the three trains, and thought that they are dozing; yet this time he didn't alert them. He went again into the forest, and asked, utilizing similar words. What's more a holy messenger from paradise came to him and invigorated him. He was presently prepared for the destiny that was soon to come, and his heart was solid. Yet again he went to the three teaches, and shared with them: "You should rest on now, and take your rest, for the hour is within reach; and as of now the son of man is given by the trickster under the control of miscreants. However, ascend and leave us alone going. It couldn't be any more obvious, the deceiver has arrived!"

The treachery

The devotees got up; they heard the commotion of a group, and saw the glimmering of lights and the sparkling of blades and lances. In the crowd they saw Judas standing, and they knew since he was the swindler of whom Jesus had spoken the prior night. Judas came surging forward, and kissed Jesus, like he was happy to see him. This was a sign that he had given in advance to the band; for the men of the watchman didn't know Jesus, and Judas had shared with them:
"The one that I will kiss is the man that you are to take; hold onto him and hold him fast." Jesus told Judas, "Judas, do you deceive the Son of man with a kiss?" Then he went to the group, and said, "Whom do you look for?"
They replied, "Jesus of Nazareth." Jesus said, "I'm he."

At the point when Jesus said this, an abrupt dread happened upon his adversaries; they moved back and fell upon the ground.
They replied, "Jesus of Nazareth." Jesus said, "I'm he."
Whenever Jesus said this, an unexpected dread happened upon his foes; they stepped back and fell upon the ground.
After a second, Jesus said once more, "Whom do you look for?" And again, they replied, "Jesus of Nazareth."
What's more Jesus said, highlighting his followers, "I let you know that I am he. Assuming you are looking for me, let these devotees head out in a different direction."

The Story of the Palm Branches

From Jericho, Jesus and his pupils went up the mountains, and came to Bethany, where his companions Martha and Mary resided, and where he had raised Lazarus to life. Many individuals in Jerusalem heard that Jesus was there, and they left the city to see him, for Bethany was just two miles from Jerusalem. Some came likewise to see Lazarus, whom Jesus had raised from the dead; however, the leaders of the Jews told one another:
"We should kill Jesus, yet Lazarus, additionally; in light of the fact that for him so many individuals are following Jesus and accept on him."
The companions of Jesus in Bethany made a dinner for Jesus, at the place of a man named Simon. He was designated "Simon the pariah"; and maybe he was one whom Jesus had restored of sickness. Jesus and his pupils, with Lazarus, inclined upon the love seats around the table, as the visitors; and Martha was one of the individuals who held up upon them. While they were at the dinner, Mary, the sister of Lazarus, came into the room, conveying a fixed container of extremely valuable aroma. She opened the container, and poured a portion of the fragrance upon the head of Jesus, and some upon his feet; and she cleaned his feet with her long hair. What's more the entire house was loaded up with the scent of the aroma.
Yet, one of the pupils of Jesus, Judas Iscariot, was not satisfied at this. He said: "Why was a particularly misuse of the aroma made? This may have been sold for more than 45 dollars, and the cash given to poor people!" This he said, yet not on the grounds that he really focused on poor people. Judas was the person who saved the pack of cash for Jesus and the twelve; and he was a hoodlum, and removed for his own utilization all the cash that he could take. Be that as it may, Jesus said:
"Leave her be; the reason does you see problem with the lady? She has accomplished a decent work upon me. You have the poor generally with you, and at whatever point you wish, you can provide for them. In any case, you will have me with you just a short time. She has done what she could; for she has come to aroma my body for its entombment. Also, really, I share with you, that any place the gospel will be lectured all through all the world, how this lady has treated be told in memory of her."

Jesus' riding into Jerusalem

Maybe Mary knew what others didn't accept, that Jesus was soon to kick the bucket; and she showed her affection for him, and her distress for his approaching passing, by this rich gift. In any case, Judas, the devotee who conveyed the sack, was exceptionally irate with Jesus; and from that time, he was searching for an opportunity to deceive Jesus, or to surrender him to his adversaries. He went to the main clerics, and said: "What will you give me, assuming I will place Jesus in your grasp?"
They said, "We will give you thirty bits of silver."
Also, for thirty bits of silver Judas vowed to assist them with taking Jesus, and make him their prisoner.
They said, "We will give you thirty pieces of silver."
Additionally for thirty pieces of silver Judas pledged to help them with taking Jesus, and make him their prisoner.
"Go into the following town, and where two streets cross; and there you will find an ass tied, and a yearling with it. Free them, and carry them to me. What's more on the off chance that any one tells you, 'For what reason do you do this?' say, 'The Lord has need of them,' and they will release them."
They went to the spot and tracked down the ass and the foal, and were losing them, when the proprietor said:
"How are you treating, the ass?"
What's more they said, as Jesus had advised them to say:
"The Lord has need of it."
Then, at that point, the proprietor gave them the ass and the yearling for the utilization of Jesus. They welcomed them to Jesus on the Mount of Olives; and they laid their very own portion garments on the yearling for a pad, and set Jesus upon it. Then, at that point, every one of the pupils and an extremely extraordinary huge number tossed their pieces of clothing upon the ground for Jesus to ride upon. Others cut down branches from the trees and laid them on the ground. Then, all of the understudies and an amazingly unprecedented immense number threw their garments upon the ground for Jesus to ride upon. Others cut down branches from the trees and laid them on the ground. What's more as Jesus' rode over the mountain toward Jerusalem, many strolled before him waving parts of palm trees. What's more they generally cried together:
"Hosanna to the child of David! Favored is he that cometh for the sake of the Master! Favored be the realm of our dad David, that cometh for the sake of the Master! Hosanna in the most elevated!"
These things they said, in light of the fact that they accepted that Jesus was the Christ, the Blessed Lord; and they trusted that he would now set up his lofty position in Jerusalem. A portion of the Pharisees in the group, who didn't put stock in Jesus, shared with him: Ace, stop your supporters!" Yet Jesus said:

"I tell you, that if these should stay composed, the very stones would shout out!"
What's more when he came into Jerusalem with this large number, all the city was loaded up with amazement. They said: "Who is this?"
Also, the large number replied:
"This is Jesus, the prophet of Nazareth in Galilee!"
Furthermore, Jesus went into the Sanctuary, and checked out it; however, he didn't remain, in light of the fact that the hour was late. He went again to Bethany, and there remained around evening time with his companions.
These things occurred on Sunday, the primary day of the week; and that Sunday in the year is called Palm Sunday, due to the palm branches that individual conveyed before Jesus.
Many individuals heard him readily, however the extraordinary city was hard of hearing to his pleadings. "O Jerusalem, Jerusalem," he cried, "thou that kills the prophets, how regularly would I have assembled thy youngsters together, even as a hen accumulates her chickens under the care of her, and ye would not!"

Jesus' riding into Jerusalem

Maybe Mary knew what others didn't accept, that Jesus was soon to bite the dust; and she showed her affection for him, and her distress for his approaching demise, by this rich gift. However, Judas, the supporter who conveyed the sack, was extremely irate with Jesus; and from that time, he was searching for an opportunity to sell out Jesus, or to surrender him to his adversaries. He went to the main ministers, and said: "What will you give me, assuming that I will place Jesus in your grasp?"

They said, "We will give you thirty bits of silver."

Also, for thirty bits of silver Judas vowed to assist them with taking Jesus, and make him their prisoner.

On the morning after the dinner at Bethany, Jesus called two of his pupils, and told them: "Go into the following town, and where two streets cross; and there you will find an ass tied, and a foal with it. Free them, and carry them to me. What's more on the off chance that any one shares with you, 'For what reason do you do this?' say, 'The Lord has need of them,' and they will release them."

They went to the spot and tracked down the ass and the yearling, and were losing them, when the proprietor said:

"How are you treating, the ass?"

Also, they said, as Jesus had advised them to say:

"The Lord has need of it."

Then, at that point, the proprietor gave them the ass and the foal for the utilization of Jesus. They welcomed them to Jesus on the Mount of Olives; and they laid their very own portion garments on the foal for a pad, and set Jesus upon it. Then at that point, every one of the followers and an extremely extraordinary large number tossed their pieces of clothing upon the ground for Jesus to ride upon. Others cut down branches from the trees and laid them on the ground. What's more as Jesus' rode over the mountain toward Jerusalem, many strolled before him waving parts of palm trees. Furthermore, they generally cried together:

"Hosanna to the child of David! Favored is he that cometh for the sake of the Lord! Favored be the realm of our dad David, that cometh for the sake of the Lord! Hosanna in the most noteworthy!"

These things they said, in light of the fact that they accepted that Jesus was the Christ, the Anointed King; and they trusted that he would now set up his lofty position in Jerusalem. A portion of the Pharisees in the group, who didn't have faith in Jesus, told him:

"Ace, stop your pupils!"

Yet, Jesus said:

"I tell you, that if these should stay composed, the very stones would shout out!"

What's more when he came into Jerusalem with this huge number, all the city was loaded up with amazement. They said: "Who is this?"

Also, the large number replied:

"This is Jesus, the prophet of Nazareth in Galilee!"

Also, Jesus went into the Temple, and checked out it; yet he didn't remain, on the grounds that the hour was late. He went again to Bethany, and there remained around evening time with his companions.

These things occurred on Sunday, the main day of the week; and that Sunday in the year is called Palm Sunday, in light of the palm branches that individual conveyed before Jesus.

Many individuals heard him readily, however the incredible city was hard of hearing to his pleadings. "O Jerusalem, Jerusalem," he cried, "thou that kills the prophets, how frequently would I have accumulated thy youngsters together, even as a hen assembles her chickens under the care of her, and ye would not!"

The Good Shepherd and the Good Samaritan

Before long subsequently Jesus provided for individuals in Jerusalem the illustration or story of "The Good Shepherd."

"Verily, verily (that is, 'in truth, in truth'), I share with you, on the off chance that any one doesn't go into the sheepfold by the entryway, however scales another way, it is an indication that he is a criminal and a burglar. Be that as it may, the person who comes in by the entryway is a shepherd of the sheep. The doorman makes the way for him, and the sheep know him, and pay attention to his call, for he calls his own sheep by name and leads them out to the field.

What's more when he has driven out his sheep, he goes before them, and the sheep follow him, for they know his voice. The sheep won't follow an outsider, for they don't have the foggiest idea about the more interesting's voice."

Individuals wasn't sure what this implied, and as Jesus disclosed it to them, he said: "Verily, verily, I say unto you, I am the entryway that prompts the sheepfold. Assuming any man comes to the sheep in some other manner than through me and in my name, he is a criminal and a looter; yet the individuals who are the genuine sheep won't hear such. I'm the entryway; assuming any man goes into the overlay through me, he will be saved, will go in and go out, and will track down field. "The cheat comes to the overlay that he might take and burglarize the sheep, and kill them; however, I came to the overlap that they might have life, and may have all that they require. I'm the great shepherd; the great shepherd will surrender his own life to save his sheep; and I will surrender my life that my sheep might be saved.

"I'm the great shepherd; and similarly, as a genuine shepherd knows all the sheep in his overlap, so I know my own, and my own know me, even as I probably am aware the father, and the father knows me; and I set out my life for the sheep. What's more other sheep I have, which are not of this crease; them additionally I should lead; and they will hear my voice; and there will be one run and one shepherd."

The Jews couldn't comprehend these expressions of Jesus; yet they ended up being exceptionally furious with him, since he talked about God as his Father. They took up stones to toss them at him, and attempted to hold onto him, planning to kill him. In any case, Jesus got away from their hands, and disappeared to the land past Jordan, at the spot called "Bethabara," or "Bethany past Jordan," a similar spot where he had been submersed by John the Baptist over two years prior. From this spot, Jesus wished to go out through the land in the east of the Jordan, a land that is classified "Perea," a word that signifies "past." But prior to going out through this land, Jesus conveyed seventy picked men from among his devotees to go to every one of the towns, and to prepare individuals for his own approaching a while later. He provided for these seventy the very orders that he had given to the twelve followers when he sent them through Galilee, and sent them out two by two, two men to make a trip and to lecture together. He said:

"I send you forward as sheep among wolves. Convey no satchel, no pack for food, no shoes aside from those that you are wearing. Try not to stop to chat with individuals coincidentally; however, go through the towns and towns, mending the wiped out, and lecturing individuals, 'The realm of God is coming,' He that hears you, hears me; and he that denies you, denies me; and he that won't hear me, won't hear him that sent me."

The Good Samaritan

What's more after a period the seventy men returned again to Jesus, saying:
Ruler, even the malicious spirits comply with our words in thy name!"
Furthermore, Jesus told them:
"I saw Satan, the lord of the abhorrent spirits, tumbling down like lightning from paradise. I have enabled you to step upon snakes and scorpions, and nothing will hurt you. All things considered, don't cheer on the grounds that the insidious spirits submit to you; yet celebrate that your names are written in paradise."
Furthermore, around then, one of the copyists' men who composed duplicates of the books of the Old Testament, and concentrated on them, and showed them-came to Jesus and posed him an inquiry, to see what answer he would give. He said: "Expert, how will I have never-ending life?"
Jesus shared with the recorder: "What is written in the law? You are a peruse of God's law; let me know what it says."
Then, at that point, the man offered this response:
"Thou shalt love the Lord thy God with all thy heart, and with all thy soul, furthermore, with all thy strength, and with all thy psyche; and thou shalt love thy neighbor as thyself."

Jesus shared with the man: "You have addressed right; do this, and you will have never-ending life."
However, the man was not fulfilled. He posed another inquiry: "And who is my neighbor?"
To address this inquiry, Jesus gave the anecdote or story of "The Good Samaritan." He said: "A specific man was going down the forlorn street from Jerusalem to Jericho; and he fell among burglars, who stripped him of all that he had and beat him; and afterward disappeared, leaving him practically dead.
It happened that a specific cleric was going down that street; and when he saw the man lying there, he passed by on the opposite side. What's more a Levite, likewise, when he came to the spot, and saw the man, he also went by on the opposite side. Yet, a specific Samaritan, as he was going down, came where this man was; and when he saw him, he had a sympathy for him. He came to the man, and dressed his injuries, emptying oil and wine into them. Then, at that point, he lifted him up, set him on his own pack animal, and strolled adjacent to him to a hotel. There he dealt with him the entire evening; and the following morning he took out from his handbag two shillings, and gave them to the guardian of the hotel, and said: 'Deal with him; and in the event that you want to spend more than this, do as such; and when I come back again, I will pay it to you.'"
The Good Samaritan at the motel

"Which one of these three, do you suppose, showed himself a neighbor to the one who fell among the looters?"

The recorder said: "The person who showed benevolence on him." Then Jesus told him: "Proceed to do thou moreover."

By this anecdote, Jesus showed that "our neighbor" is the person who needs the assist that we with canning give him, whoever he might be.

The Story of the Miracle Worker

There was at Capernaum an official of the Roman armed force, a man who had under him an organization of 100 men. They referred to him as "a centurion," a word that signifies "directing 100"; however, we should refer to him as "a commander." This man was not a Jew, but rather was what the Jews called "a Gentile," "an outsider"; a name which the Jews provided for all individuals outside their own race. The whole world with the exception of the actual Jews were Gentiles.

This Roman centurion was a decent man, and he cherished the Jews, in light of the fact that through them he had known about God, and had figured out how to love God. Out of his affection for the Jews, he had worked for them with his own cash a place of worship, which might have been the very temple wherein Jesus educated on the Sabbath days.

The centurion had a youthful worker, a kid whom he cherished extraordinarily; and this kid was exceptionally debilitated with paralysis, and close ridiculously. The centurion had heard that Jesus could fix the people who were debilitated; and he requested the main men from the place of worship, who were referred to it as "elderly folks," to go to Jesus and request that he come and fix his young worker.

The elderly folks addressed Jesus, similarly as he returned again to Capernaum, after the Sermon on the Mount. They requested that Jesus go with them to the centurion's home; and they said:

"He is a commendable man, and it is fitting that you should help him, for, however a Gentile, he cherishes our kin, and he has worked for us our place of worship."

Then, at that point, Jesus said, "I will proceed to recuperate him."

Yet, while he was coming and with him were the seniors, and his devotees, and an incredible horde of individuals, who expected to see crafted by recuperating the centurion sent a few different companions to Jesus with this message:

"Master, don't go out of the way to come to my home; for I am not commendable that one so exceptionally high as you are should gone under my rooftop; and I didn't feel that I

was qualified to proceed to address you.

. In any case, express just a word where you are and my worker will be made well. For I likewise am a man under rule, and I have troopers under me; and I tell one 'Go,' and he goes; and to another, 'Come,' and he comes; and to my worker, 'Do this,' and he makes it happen. You, as well, have ability to talk and to be complied. Express the word, and my worker will be restored."

At the point when Jesus heard this, he stood amazed at this present man's confidence. He went to individuals following him, and said:

"In truth I share with you, I have not tracked down such confidence as this in all Israel!" Then, at that point, he addressed the companions of the centurion who had brought the word from him:

"Proceed to tell this man, 'As you have put stock in me, so will it be done to you.'"

Then, at that point, the individuals who had been sent, went again to the centurion's home, and observed that in that very hour his worker had been made completely well. On the day after this, Jesus with his followers and many individuals went out from Capernaum, turned toward the south, and came to a town called Nain. Similarly, as Jesus and his supporters drew close to the entryway of the city, they were met by an organization who were doing a dead man to be covered. He was a youngster, and the main child of his mom, and she was a widow.

At the point when the Lord Jesus saw the mother in her pain, he felt sorry for her, and said, "Don't sob."

He moved close, and contacted the edge on which they were conveying the body, wrapped all around with long pieces of material. The carriers looked with wonder on this more unusual, put down the casing with its body, stopped. Remaining alongside the body, Jesus said:

"Youngster, I share with you, Rise up!"

Also in a second, the youngster sat up and started to talk. Jesus gave him to his mom, who presently saw that her child, who had been dead, was alive once more.

What's more in a second, the youngster sat up and started to talk. Jesus gave him to his mom, who currently saw that her child, who had been dead, was alive once more.

Also, Jesus went through all that piece of Galilee, working wonders, lecturing, and educating in every one of the towns, telling individuals wherever the uplifting news of the realm of God.

The youngsters wanted to assemble around him, and when his followers would have driven them away, he said, "Experience the small kids to come unto me and disallow them not, for of such is the realm of paradise."

Jesus recuperating the visually impaired man

One Sabbath day, as Jesus and his followers were strolling in Jerusalem, they met a visually impaired man asking. This man in for his entire life had never seen; for he had been conceived blind. The devotees told Jesus as they were passing him: "Expert, whose shortcoming was it that this man was conceived blind? Was this being on the grounds that he has trespassed, or did his folks sin?"

For the Jews felt that when any evil came, it was brought about by somebody's transgression. However, Jesus said:

"This man was conceived visually impaired, not due to his folks' transgression, nor as his very own result, yet with the goal that God may show his power in him. We should go about God's responsibilities while it is day, for the night is coming when no man can work. However long I am on the planet, I am the illumination of the world."

At the point when Jesus had said this, he spat on the ground, and stirred up the saliva with earth, making a little chunk of mud.

. This earth Jesus spread on the eyes of the visually impaired man; and afterward he told him: "Go wash in the pool of Siloam." The pool of Siloam was an enormous storage, or, supply, on the southeast of Jerusalem, outside the divider, where the valley of Gihon and the valley of Kedron meet up. To go to this pool, the visually impaired man, with two extraordinary blotches of mud all over, should stroll through the roads of the city, out of the door, and into the valley. He went, and felt his direction down the means into the pool of Siloam. There he washed, and afterward without a moment's delay his deep-rooted visual deficiency died, and he could see.

At the point when the man returned to the area of the city where he resided, his neighbors could hardly accept that he was a similar man. They said: "Isn't this the one who used to sit on the road asking?"

"This should be a similar man," said some; yet others said: "No, it is somebody who appears as though him."

However, the man said, "I'm exactly the same man who was visually impaired!"

"Why, how did this happen?" they inquired. "How were your eyes opened?"

"For man, named Jesus," he replied, "blended dirt, and set it on my eyes, and told me, 'Go to the pool of Siloam and wash,' and I proceeded to wash, and afterward I could see."

"Where is this man?" they asked him. "I don't have the foggiest idea," said the man.

A portion of the Pharisees, the ones who made a demonstration of continuously complying with the law, asked the man how he had been made to see. He shared with them, as he had said previously:

"For man set mud on my eyes, and I washed, and my sight came to me." Some of the Pharisees said:

"The one who did this isn't a righteous man, since he doesn't keep the Sabbath. He makes dirt, and places it on men's eyes, dealing with the Sabbath day. He is a miscreant!"

Others said, "How could a man who is a miscreant do such brilliant works?"

Also subsequently, individuals were separated in what they considered Jesus. They asked the one who had been visually impaired: "How treat consider this man who has woken up?"

"He is a prophet of God," said the man.

Yet, the main Jews would not really accept that that this man had acquired his sight, until they had sent for his dad and his mom. The Jews asked them:

"Is this your child, who you say was conceived blind? How could it be that he can now see?"

His folks were reluctant to tell all they knew; for the Jews had concurred that assuming any man should say Jesus was the Christ, the Savior, he ought to be turned out of the gathering place, and not be permitted to adore anything else with individuals. So, his folks told the Jews:

"We realize that this is our child, and we realize that he was conceived blind. In any case, how he was made to see, we don't have the foggiest idea; or who has woken up, we don't have the foggiest idea. He is old enough; ask him, and allow him to represent himself."

Of course, the leaders of the Jews called the one who had been visually impaired; and they shared with him:
"Give God the recognition for your sight. We realize that this man who made dirt on the Sabbath day is a delinquent."
"Regardless of whether that man is a delinquent, or not, I don't have the foggiest idea," addressed the man; "however one thing I do know, that once I was visually impaired, and presently I see. We realize that God doesn't hear delinquents; yet God hears just the individuals who love him, and do his will. Never before has any one opened the eyes of a man conceived blind. On the off chance that this man was not from God, he was unable to do such functions as these!"
The leaders of the Jews, these Pharisees, then, at that point, told the man: "You were brought into the world in transgression, and do you attempt to instruct us?"
What's more they turned him out of the place of worship, and would not allow anybody to venerate with him. Jesus knew about this; and when Jesus observed him, he shared with him:
"Do you accept on the Son of God?"
The man said:
"What's more who is he, Lord, that I might accept on him?"
"You have seen him," said Jesus, "and it is he who presently chats with you!" The man said, "Ruler, I accept."
Also, he tumbled down before Jesus, and venerated him.

The Story of the Sermon on the Mount

Among the Jews there was one class of men loathed and detested by individuals more than some other. That was "the publicans." These were the ones who took from individuals the assessment that the Roman rulers had laid upon the land. A large number of these publicans were egotistical, getting a handle on, and brutal. They ransacked individuals, taking more than was correct. Some of them were straightforward men, managing reasonably, and taking no more for the assessment than was needful; but since so many were underhanded, every one of the publicans were despised the same; and they were classified "delinquents" by individuals.
At some point, when Jesus was leaving Capernaum, to the shoreline, trailed by an incredible horde of individuals, he passed a publican, or duty finder, who was situated at his table taking cash from individuals who came to make good on their expenses. This man was named Matthew, or Levi; for some, Jews had two names.
Jesus could investigate the hearts of men, and he saw that Matthew was one who may help him as one of his supporters. He viewed Matthew, and said:
"Follow me!"
Immediately, the publican ascended from his table, and passed on it to go with Jesus.

Every one individual pondered, as they saw one of the detested publicans among the

followers, with Peter, and John, and the rest. Yet, Jesus accepted that there is great in a wide range of individuals.

The majority of the ones who followed him were helpless anglers. Not even one of them, supposedly, was rich. What's more when he called Matthew, he saw a man with a valid and cherishing heart, who's ascending to follow Jesus' right when he was called showed what a courageous and devoted companion he would be. The first of the four books about Jesus bears Matthew's name.

A short time after Jesus called him, Matthew made an extraordinary dining experience for Jesus at his home; and to the banquet he welcomed numerous publicans, and others whom the Jews called heathens. The Pharisees saw Jesus sitting among these individuals, and they said with contempt to his pupils:

"For what reason does your Master find a seat at the table with publicans and delinquents?" Jesus knew about what these men had said, and he said:

"Those that are well needn't bother with a specialist to fix them, however those that are wiped out do require one. I go to these individuals since they realize that they are heathens and should be saved. I came not to call the people who believe themselves to be great, yet the individuals who wish to be improved."

One evening Jesus went alone to a mountain not a long way from Capernaum. A horde of individuals and his devotees followed him; yet Jesus left them all, and went up to the highest point of the mountain, where he could be separated from everyone else. There he remained the entire evening, imploring God, his Father and our Father. Toward the beginning of the day, out of the entirety of his adherents, he picked twelve men who should stroll with him and pay attention to his words, so they could possibly show others thulian. A portion of the men he had called previously; yet presently he called them once more, and others with them. They were classified "The Twelve," or "the devotees"; and after Jesus went to paradise, they were designated "The Apostles," a word which signifies "the individuals who were conveyed," in light of the fact that Jesus sent them out to lecture the gospel to the world

The names of the twelve devotees, or witnesses, were these: Simon Peter and his sibling Andrew; James and John, the two children of Zebedee; Philip of Bethsaida, and Nathanael, who was additionally called Bartholomew, a name which signifies "the child of Thalami"; Thomas, who was likewise called Didymus, a name which signifies "a twin," and Matthew the publican, or assessment finder; another James, the child of Alpheus, who was classified "James the Less," to keep his name separated from the principal James, the sibling of John; and Lebbeus, who was additionally called Thaddeus. Lebbeus was additionally called Judas, however he was an alternate man from another Judas, whose name is given last all of the time. The 11th name was another Simon, who was classified "the Cunanan" or "Simon Zelotes"; and the last name was Judas Iscariot, who was thereafter the trickster. We know very little about a large portion of these men, yet some of them in later days accomplished an incredible work. Simon Peter was a pioneer among them, however the majority of them were normal kind of men of whom the best we know is that they cherished Jesus and followed him as far as possible. Some kicked the bucket for him, and a few served him in far off and risky spots.

Before every one individual who had come to hear him, Jesus called these twelve men to remain close by. Then, at that point, on the mountain, he lectured these followers and to the extraordinary organization of individuals. The followers remained alongside him, and the incredible horde of individuals remained in front, while Jesus talked. What he said on that day is designated "The Sermon on the Mount." Matthew recorded it, and you can peruse it in his gospel, in the fifth, 6th, and seventh sections. Jesus started with these words to his devotees:

"Favored are the poor in soul: for theirs is the realm of paradise. "Favored are they that grieve: for they will be ameliorated. "Favored are the resigned: for they will acquire basically everything.

"Favored are they which in all actuality do craving and yearn for nobility: for they will be filled.

"Favored are the kind: for they will acquire benevolence. "Favored are the unadulterated in heart: for they will see God.

"Favored are the peacemakers: for they will be known as the offspring of God. "Favored are they which are mistreated for the wellbeing of honesty: for theirs
is the realm of paradise.

"Favored are ye when men will scold you, and aggrieve you, and will say all way of evil against you dishonestly, for the wellbeing of I.

"Cheer, and be really happy: for incredible is your prize in paradise: for so mistreated they the prophets which were before you.

"Ye are the good and honest: however, on the off chance that the salt has lost his relish, wherewith will it be salted? It is thereupon deadbeat, yet to be projected out, and to be trampled on the ground of men.

"Ye are the radiance of the world. A city that is set on a slope can't be stowed away. Neither do men light a flame, and put it under a bushel, however on a candle; and it gives light unto all that are in the house. Allow your light so to sparkle before men, that they might see your benevolent acts, and extol your father which is in paradise."

It was in this Sermon on the Mount that Jesus let individuals know how they ought to implore, and he gave them the petition that we as a whole known as the Lord's Prayer. Also, this was the finish of the Sermon:

"In this way, whosoever hears these expressions of mine, and does them, I will compare him unto a savvy man, which fabricated his home upon a stone:

"Furthermore, the downpour plunged, and the floods came, and the breezes blew, and beat upon that house; and it fell not; for it was established upon a stone.

"What's more every one that hears these adages of mine, and doeth them not, will be compared unto a stupid man, which constructed his home upon the sand:

"What's more the downpour slipped, and the floods came, and the breezes blew, and beat upon that house; and it fell: and extraordinary was its fall."

Jesus Calms the Tempest

At one time when Jesus had entered a boat to cross the Sea of Galilee with His educates, an incredible tempest emerged and the waves almost covered the little vessel, so they were obviously in extraordinary peril. The pupils were scared; however, Jesus was sleeping and the tempest didn't upset Him. As it deteriorated and more terrible and the followers turned out to be like never before apprehensive, they returned to where Jesus lay and aroused Him, shouting out, "Expert, dost Thou not mind that we die?"

At the point when they said this, Jesus emerged and addressed the breezes and the ocean, saying, "Harmony, stay composed!" Then without a moment's delay the breeze went down and the ocean became quiet, and the hearts of the men were loaded up with amazement and still more prominent confidence and wonderment, while they told each other, "What way of man is this, that even the breeze and the ocean submit to Him?" They had not yet discovered that Jesus had control over all things at whatever point He decided to practice it.

Jesus quiets the whirlwind

At some other point when the pupils had crossed the Sea of Galilee, expecting that Jesus would go along with them upon the opposite side, a tempest came up, unexpectedly as in the past, and the waters were immediately stacked up in extraordinary waves; for the lake was restricted and profound, and the tempests normally burst in full fierceness with minimal notice, causing a lot of damage before there was an opportunity to get away. Right now, the pupils had difficult work to push the boat against the breeze, and it was thrown about to a great extent by the waves in the ocean until, toward morning, Jesus went out toward it, strolling upon the water.
Jesus strolling on the water
At the point when the followers saw Him coming, they thought it was a soul and were terrified: however, He addressed them, saying, "Be happy; it is I, be not apprehensive."

Feeding the Multitudes

Jesus had picked twelve out of the numerous who ran about Him wishing to be His pupils, and these twelve were called witnesses. He sent them forward to lecture the gospel, enabling them to project out detestable spirits and to recuperate illnesses; and when they were going to go forward upon their central goal, He gave them directions with respect to how they were to treat, cautioned them of the mistreatments which would be piled upon them. He additionally bade them be solid and not dread the people who had ability to kill the body just, in light of the fact that the spirit was undeniably more valuable. So, the messengers went out into the urban areas and towns, lectured the expression of God, and conveyed favoring with them. At the point when they returned, they let Jesus know how they had treated, they went with Him across the Sea of Galilee to a calm place where they could rest and talk over their work.

In any case, individuals circumvented the ocean, or lake, to go along with them on the opposite side; and when Jesus saw the groups, He was upset for them, and instructed and mended them again as He had done as such commonly.

Jesus showing the hoards

In the evening His pupils asked Him to send individuals away that they may purchase nourishment for themselves in the town; yet Jesus said, "Give ye them to eat." The devotees thought this sounds unimaginable at least in theory. "We have here however five portions and two fishes," they told Him; and when He said, "Bring them here to Me," they submitted to Him with amazement.

Then, at that point, Jesus directed individuals to plunk down in bunches upon the green grass; and He took the portions and expressed appreciation to God for them, and broke them.

into pieces, giving them to His supporters to provide for individuals.

He partitioned the fishes likewise similarly, the supporters went about among the gatherings giving every individual an offer, and everybody had enough to eat; for despite the fact that there were around 5,000 men there, other than ladies and kids, the food was adequate for all. Significantly more than this, when the large number had eaten all that, they needed, the supporters got together twelve bins loaded with the messed-up pieces.

Whenever individuals saw this superb marvel which Jesus had done, they wished to make Him lord immediately, for they thought He was the Promised One for whom they had been for such a long time pausing, and they didn't realize that the realm of Christ was not to be a natural realm.

However, Jesus would not permit them to make Him ruler, and He left them and went up on the highest point of a mountain alone.

On one more event when an incredible group had accumulated to hear Him and had been for quite a while without food, He called His devotees to Him and let them know that He felt extremely upset for individuals since they had been fasting three days, and He was unable to send them away so feeble and hungry for dread they would black out before they could arrive at home.

Yet, His followers said they didn't have any idea where they could get nourishment for so many, as they were in the wild.

Jesus requested them the number of portions from bread they had, and they let him know seven, and a couple of little fishes.

Then, at that point, Jesus bade individuals plunk down on the ground around Him, and He took the seven portions and the fishes and offered because of God; thereafter, He broke the portions into pieces as He had done previously and gave them, with the fishes, to His devotees, and the followers appropriated them among individuals. As they gave out the food it kept on expanding superbly, so everyone individuals were taken care of; and surprisingly after that there was food enough left so they took up seven bushels full, albeit around 4,000 men, with numerous ladies and youngsters, had eaten.

These wonders show the force of our Lord, yet His delicacy and care for people around Him in the ordinary undertakings of life. He not just focused on the spirits of His kin, however for their actual solace also; for His heart was at any point open to the call of human need.

One of the principal acts by which He showed His capacity to the ones who a short time later turned into His followers, was a demonstration of supportiveness.

He saw two boats by the Lake of Gennesaret with the anglers close by

washing their nets, and getting on one of the boats, which had a place with Simon Peter, He requested that he put out a little way from land; then, at that point, when His solicitation had been consented to, He showed individuals from the boat.

After He had completed His instructing, He shared with Simon, "Jump start out into the profound and let down your nets for a draft." Simon let him know that they had worked the entire evening and had gotten no fish, however that they would do as He bade them.

Furthermore, when they had done as such, the net was filled with the goal that it broke, and they needed to call to their accomplices in the other boat to come and help them; and the two boats were filled. Then, at that point, Peter, James, and John passed on all to follow Jesus.

THE END

www.ingramcontent.com/pod-product-compliance
Lightning Source LLC
LaVergne TN
LVHW081526060526
838200LV00044B/2013